D1373925

THE TEACHER AND
THE MACHINE

HORACE MANN LECTURE

1967

THE TEACHER AND
THE MACHINE

By

PHILIP W. JACKSON

Professor of Education and Human Development
University of Chicago

LIBRARY OF CONGRESS CATALOG
CARD NO. 68–12729

HORACE MANN LECTURES

THE HORACE MANN LECTURESHIP

To commemorate the life of Horace Mann, 1796-1859, and in recognition of his matchless services to the American Public School System, the School of Education of the University of Pittsburgh, in cooperation with the Tri-State Area School Study Council, established the Horace Mann Lectureship. The striking and varied contributions of Horace Mann must ever be kept alive and be reemphasized in each generation. It is difficult, indeed, to assess the magnitude of Mann's educational services. Turning from the profession of law, he devoted his life to the study and improvement of education. He, more than any other, can truly be called "Father of the American Public School System." His boundless energy, coupled with a brilliant and penetrating mind, focused the attention of the citizens of his era on the need for the improvement and support of public schools. His services were manifold. It shall be the pur-

POSE OF THESE LECTURES TO REAFFIRM HIS FAITH IN FREE SCHOOLS AND TO CALL TO THEIR SERVICE ALL CITIZENS OF THIS GENERATION. IT IS VITAL THAT ALL UNDERSTAND THE PURPOSE AND FUNCTION OF A FREE PUBLIC SCHOOL SYSTEM IN AMERICAN DEMOCRACY.

THE HORACE MANN LECTURES ARE PUBLISHED ANNUALLY BY THE UNIVERSITY OF PITTSBURGH PRESS.

To Francis S. Chase
—with gratitude and admiration

ACKNOWLEDGMENT

This essay began as a paper prepared for the Committee for Economic Development in 1966. Although the present version is much longer than the original and contains many important changes, I have retained the title, "The Teacher and the Machine," because it continues to describe the central topic around which my argument revolves. I am grateful to the officials of the Committee for Economic Development for their initial encouragement and for their permission to use the title and selected portions of the earlier manuscript.

THE TEACHER AND
THE MACHINE

The Teacher and the Machine

THE ARGUMENT contained in this essay is divided into three parts: first, that changes in the teacher's work resulting from the growth of educational technology will not be as dramatic, and will not occur as rapidly, as many of the headline-making predictions would have us believe; second, that several of the educational benefits alleged to accompany technological change will either fail to materialize or, at best, will prove to be mixed blessings; third, that although the expanded use of machines in the classroom poses some unique problems for educators, a more fundamental question concerns the extent to which a mechanistic ideology should be allowed to permeate our view of the educational process.

A year or so ago, while attending a research conference on teaching, I was chided by a colleague to whom I had described my interest in observing teachers in action. Watching live teachers is a waste of the researcher's time, he argued, especially since, in the future, many of the teacher's present tasks will be eliminated. My trouble, he warned—with a burst of metaphor—was that I was doing research on oil lamps in an age that had discovered the light bulb!

The educational light bulb, in my friend's view, is the computer-based auto-instructional device, but equally dramatic comparisons have been advanced to herald the impact of mechanical teaching machines, airborne television, instructional films, and, if we go back far enough, the humble crystal set. These predictions typically erupt in the heat of a discussion and no one is expected to take them too seriously. Judging from the passion and the frequency with which such views are expressed, however, a great many people apparently are deeply convinced that a new educational era is dawning. Some of them, one suspects, can hardly wait for it to come. Radical advocates of what has been called "the technological revolution in education" seem to look forward to the time when they can say, "Goodby, Mr. Chips, and good riddance!" Others, equally convinced of the inevitability of change, await with chilling apprehension the day when classrooms are bedecked with signs reminding students to turn their teacher off before they leave the room.

Although it is foolhardy to counter one set of predictions with another, since future events have a way of eluding prior description, there is reason to suspect that many of the bolder forecasts concerning technological change in education will not be fulfilled. If these predictions do fail to come true, that failure will be due, in part, to the existence of powerful conservative forces within the school, forces operating to thwart certain technological innovations, or at least to retard their development. These retarding influences, which arise in part from the teaching process itself and in part from the personal qualities of those who choose to work in the schools, must be examined as we think about the changing demands that will face tomorrow's teacher.

As it is typically conducted, teaching is an opportunistic process. That is to say, neither the teacher nor the student can predict with any great accuracy exactly what will happen next. Plans are forever going awry and unexpected opportunities for the achievement of specific goals continually emerge. Stray thoughts, sudden insights, meandering digressions, irrelevant asides, and other unpredicted events constantly ruffle the smoothness of the instructional dialogue. In most classrooms, as every teacher knows, the path of educational progress could be more easily traced by a butterfly than by a bullet. Seasoned teachers accept this state of affairs and even come to relish the elements of surprise and uncertainty that make up an integral part of their work.

Would-be critics of live teaching must understand that the unpredictable quality of classroom activity cannot be looked upon as just another sign of human fallibility, a product of poor planning on the part of the teacher. Moreover, the causes of these disruptions in plans can only be eliminated at great cost to the naturalness of the teaching encounter, for they are part and parcel of the human situation. That is, they reflect the normal fluctuations and mutations of man's thinking and feeling. Interesting activities grow dull, boring discussions come to life, unintelligible explanations emerge into clarity, the skills mastered yesterday are falteringly executed today. We must be exceedingly cautious in interpreting these changes as evidence of good or poor pedagogy. It is more accurate to think of them as the facts of life with which the teacher must work.

The unpredictability of human behavior necessitates flexibility in educational planning. If the unexpected is bound to happen, the teacher had better be prepared to deal with it. This means having on hand instructional tools that can be readily adapted to a wide variety of educational tasks. Indeed, the criterion of adaptability is so important that the more flexible a technique or piece of teaching equipment, the more likely it is to be adopted by teachers. Blackboards and books provide good examples of this important quality.

The blackboard is literally at the teacher's

fingertips. He can write on it, draw on it, immediately erase what he has written, or preserve it for days. He can scrawl key words on it, produce a detailed diagram, or write out a series of essay questions. He can use the board himself, or ask his students to use it. He can place material on it in advance, or use it to capture the fleeting thoughts emerging from a discussion. Given this flexibility, it is no wonder that the chalksmudged sleeve has become the trademark of the teacher.

The book, too, is an extremely versatile tool. It is portable, compact, and enduring. It can be read for a few minutes at a time or for many hours at a stretch. It can be studied carefully or skimmed quickly; read once or reread often. All students can be given the same reading assignment or each can be given a different one. They can all move through the material at the same pace or at very different speeds. The reader can proceed methodically from the beginning to the end of the book or he can move back and forth from one section to another. He can skip unimportant passages or linger contentedly over a well-written paragraph. He can use his book in class, at home, or in the library. If he wishes, he can even sprawl out on the grass with text in hand.

These obvious virtues of blackboards and books provide a standard of flexibility against which mechanized teaching devices can be compared. Almost all of these devices, from filmstrips to video tapes and from programmed texts to computer-based instructional systems, require much more planning and, hence, introduce greater rigidity to the teaching program than do the standard tools of chalk and printed page. Admittedly, the newer devices do have distinct advantages for certain instructional purposes, but they create added difficulties as well.

Films must be ordered in advance and often must be returned after one or two viewings; live television broadcasts must be viewed at a special time or missed completely; the use of machine facilities requires careful scheduling; students' absences and tardiness compound these difficulties. The results are often worth the extra trouble, to be sure. For many instructional purposes a picture is indeed worth a thousand words, and a moving picture is often more valuable than reams of textbook exposition. Clearly, certain kinds of educational experiences can only be achieved with the aid of these devices. But these advantages are almost invariably accompanied by a loss of administrative flexibility.

The inflexibility accompanying the use of most mechanized devices in the classroom has an effect not only on the amount of time teachers must spend planning their work and the difficulties they might have in previewing materials, but also on the character of the teaching process itself. Take, as an instance, the speed and directionality of instruction. Mechanical teaching devices usually move material in one direction at a time, at a speed over which the user has only limited control. The student has no chance to say "Wait a minute!" or "Repeat that, please," when a film showing is in progress. True, the teacher might sense his difficulty and decide to show the film twice or rerun selected portions of it, but the propitious moment for clarification, when interest is high and the source of uncertainty sharply defined, may be missed.

Even when the film or the programmed material has fulfilled its instructional purpose, there is no guarantee that nothing has been lost in the process. For one thing, the serendipitous quality of human thinking is almost bound to be ignored. The student who senses a relationship between a problem in mathematics and the state of world affairs is unlikely to have his insight rewarded by the machine. Indeed, if he spends too long musing over such an "irrelevancy" he may never get through his assignment before the power is turned off for the day, or before it is someone else's turn to take his place at the console. Better push the button for the next frame and get on with it. In other words, during a mechanized display of learning materials the student must stay "on the track." He must not allow his mind to wander. Thoughts and reactions bearing only a tangential relationship to the task at hand have little place in such encounters.

We know, of course, that many teachers dislike tangential remarks from their students and do their best to keep the instructional dialogue within narrow limits. But even the most determined teacher is rarely successful in this endeavor and the modest amount of digression that seeps inevitably into a lesson likely provides a greater opportunity for exploratory thought than is possible under conditions of mechanized presentation. Under the control of a machine (or of a teacher who behaves like one) the unsystematic and often alogical quality of spontaneous interaction is all but eliminated and the opportunistic quality of the teaching process is thereby diminished.

Here, then, is one reason why many teachers find it difficult to become excited over the assortment of gadgets proffered as aids to their work. Instead of aiding them, the machine often turns out to be more trouble than it is worth. It should come as no surprise, therefore, to find that teachers have resisted the placement of these devices in their classrooms. Moreover, there is every indication that this resistence will continue despite heightened appeals from advocates of the newer media.

But the problems of scheduling and the difficulty of learning how to operate a 16mm projector or how to load an auto-instructional device are not sufficient to account for the widespread neutrality, if not open distaste, of many teachers toward the new world of educational technology. Evidence of these negative attitudes is abundant. For example, one study reported in 1962 found that only about one-fifth of a national sample of elementary school teachers had a favorable attitude toward teaching machines.[1] A more recent study documents widespread resistance among elementary school teachers to the adoption of audio-visual aids.[2] In yet a third series of investigations, groups of teachers who were attending graduate courses in education were asked to rate a set of terms describing some of the newer technological innovations (e.g., teaching machine, programmed instruction, automated instruc-

1. L. M. Stolurow, "Implications of current research and future trends," *J. of Educational Research,* 55: 519–27 (June-July 1962).

2. G. Eicholz and E. M. Rogers, "Resistance to the adoption of audio-visual aids by elementary school teachers: contrasts and similarities to agricultural innovation," in *Innovations in Education,* ed. Mathew B. Miles, New York: Bureau of Publications, Teachers College, Columbia U., 1964, pp. 194-316.

tion) along several bipolar scales (e.g., good-bad, worthless-valuable, reputable-disreputable).[3, 4] These ratings were compared with similar ratings assigned a set of terms describing "traditional practices" (e.g., exercise books, flashcard, workbook). Almost invariably the teachers responded more favorably to the traditional terms. Moreover, the favorability of the ratings did not seem to be related to the amount of familiarity the teachers had with the devices in question, nor did it seem to change after concerted efforts to "improve" the teachers' attitudes.

The pervasiveness and tenacity of these attitudes made it appear that the teachers' reluctance to use mechanical aids in the classroom springs from deeper sources than those having to do with the extra trouble and inflexibility connected with the logistics of machine use. One explanation, especially popular in some quarters, is that teachers, like the

3. S. Tobias, "Teachers' attitudes toward programed instructional terms," *J. of Programed Instruction*, 2: 25–29, 1963.

4. S. Tobias, "Lack of knowledge and fear of automation as factors in teachers' attitudes toward programed instruction and other media," *AV Communication Rev.*, 14: 99–109 (Spring 1966).

industrial workers of the last century, view with suspicion and alarm the introduction of labor-saving devices that might someday displace the human worker. This view holds, in short, that teachers do not want to lose their jobs, hence their conservatism in matters pertaining to technological advances. Although a tendency toward self-preservation may indeed color the thinking of teachers, it is not sufficiently strong, in my opinion, to serve as the foundation of their anti-machine attitudes. For one thing, the threat of mechanized instruction is not yet real enough to arouse widespread concern. Although most teachers probably have heard popular accounts describing teaching machines or computer-assisted instruction, a very small number have ever seen such devices in action. The day of the machine, if it is ever to have its day, must seem a long way off to the average classroom teacher. Surely he does not lie awake at night worrying about the pink slip that might show up in his pay envelope on the day the "hardware" arrives. Besides, he is on tenure.

Coupled with the improbability of any

swift take-over are the assurances of the machine promoters themselves, who have gone
out of their way to make it clear that they do
not have any such intentions in the first place.
Their avowed goal is not to displace teachers
but rather, to help them do their jobs more
effectively. Although a few zealots may har-
bor more nefarious schemes, only the cynic
could doubt the overall genuineness of the
technologist's desire to lend a helping hand.

If teachers do not feel themselves to be
seriously threatened by the encroachment of
technology, why do they not respond more
positively to the advances that have already
been made? If the technologist is really of-
fering a helping hand, why don't the teachers reach out more eagerly to grasp it? The
answer to such questions would seem to re-
side, in part, in ideological differences between the two groups involved. In a very
fundamental sense the world view of many
teachers, particularly of those who work in
the lower grades, is incompatible with the
view of those who serve as the spokesmen of
educational technology. Indeed, the differences between these two ways of thinking,

one characterizing the producers of many mechanical devices and the other characterizing their potential users, have important implications for the future of education.

Many of the technological tools now being designed for use in the schools are being promoted by men who talk and think like engineers. The teaching machine is a good case in point. To its promoters, the machine has a great logical appeal. Here, at last, is an invention that promises to reduce error, increase efficiency, speed learning, cut manpower costs, and ultimately transform teaching from something resembling black magic into an applied science. Anyone in his right mind, the advocates of the machine reason, will certainly recognize these virtues and applaud the device that makes them possible. When confronted with evidence of teachers' disinterest in this pedagogical miracle, the technician is often surprised, if not a bit annoyed. He wants to know what is wrong with the teachers, that they do not recognize a good thing when they see it. Perhaps a program of in-service training might remedy the situation. What the technician and his sup-

porters often do not realize is that the problem is not simply the result of teachers' lack
of information. Nor does it arise from the
alleged intellectual inferiority of teachers as
a group. Instead it has to do with the teacher's attitudes toward his work and the world
in general.

If there is one thing the teacher, particularly the female teacher, is not, it is an engineer. Indeed, it is difficult to think of two
viewpoints further apart than those symbol-
ized by the Golden Rule on the one hand
and the slide rule on the other. The one calls
to mind adjectives such as romantic, warm,
tender, naïve; while the other evokes the
concepts of realism, coldness, toughness, efficiency. One is essentially feminine, the other
masculine. These two lists undoubtedly ex-
aggerate the real differences to be found between these two groups, but they do give us
pause when we consider the likelihood of
increasing the dialogue between the tender-
minded teachers and the tough-minded technicians. To say that they do not speak the
same language is a gross understatement.

Teachers, particularly those who work

with young children, are not overly enthusiastic about the engineer's talk of speed, efficiency, accuracy, and economy. They appreciate the desirability of these qualities for technicians who are building a bridge or sending an astronaut to the moon, but, in the teacher's view, the management of a human learner requires a very different set of considerations. Although time can be wasted in school, and subjects can be taught with greater or lesser efficiency, accuracy, and economy, these are not the teacher's prime concerns. He is chiefly interested in the appropriateness of his professional actions to the unique set of circumstances confronting him and his students. He wants to do what is right at each classroom moment, but his goal is to achieve a general effect—such as his pupils' involvement in a task—and only secondarily to conserve time and energy in the process.

The casualness of the teacher's regard for these time-honored virtues must seem sacrilegious to the more militant advocates of educational engineering. To their ears, any questioning of the universal goodness of technology likely sounds almost as heretical as an attack upon the sanctity of God, Mother, and Country. And, from an engineering perspective, the charge of heresy would be entirely appropriate if teachers were themselves engaged in the design and construction of machines. A mechanical contrivance whose properties do not conform as much as possible to the cardinal virtues of the engineering sciences comes close to deserving the label: "sinful." At the very least, such contraptions might serve as the occasion for a good laugh. One has only to think of Rube Goldberg's silly inventions to realize how ludicrous it is to build a machine that takes the long way around to accomplish its ends.

But teachers are *not* engaged in the design, construction, and repair of machines, no matter how appealing the analogies that can be drawn between their work and that of the engineers. It is true that teachers do find such concepts as goal, objective, progress, and product useful in their occupational framework. It is also true that teachers may sometimes feel as if they are manipulating students toward desired ends. But what we often fail to appreciate is that the referents of these physicalistic terms lack the objectivity they generally have when they appear in the engineer's lexicon. Moreover, this lack of objectivity is not just the result of fuzzy thinking, nor can it be remedied by short courses on how to write behavioral objectives. The inexactness of the teacher's language during those moments when he talks like an engineer is simply a reflection of the fact that almost all physicalistic terms, when used to describe social affairs, have greater metaphoric than literal meaning. Teachers may talk *as if* they were heading toward concrete goals, *as if* they had clearly defined objectives, *as if* they were out to produce a tangible product. But when we press for greater specificity, when we reach for the reality behind the language, it either eludes our grasp or turns out to be quite different from that which the language suggests.

At this point the critic is apt to become impatient and insist that the teacher's orientation more closely resembles that of the engineer than this discussion would have it seem. After all, he might ask, is it not true that teachers want their students to learn specific skills and to master specific content? Billy does have to know how to read and write and spell and figure. Surely every third grader ought to know who Christopher Columbus was, and every teenager ought to have some acquaintance with the events leading up to the Revolutionary War. What are these if not specific objectives toward which the teacher guides his students? And as long as they can be identified, what is wrong with moving toward them speedily, and with a minimum of wasted motion? Think of how much more could be accomplished if we increased our educational efficiency.

The weakness of this argument, in addition to its oversimplification, is its tendency to confuse the molar and the molecular aspects of the teacher's role. In so doing, it makes the error of assuming that the global goals of the teacher are ultimately reducible to a set of specific objectives, and further, that the teacher's concern with his students' progress ought to focus on the conditions

surrounding the attainment of these frag-
mented objectives. This is not the way most
teachers view their task. Instead, they seem
to take a more holistic view. They worry
more about whether a student is learning
how to read than whether he is still confus-
ing "saw" and "was." They are more concerned with seeing satisfactory progress in
arithmetic than with the mastery of any
specific number fact. Their focus, in other
words, is on broad constellations of compe-
tencies, the components of which may be de-
veloping at different rates for different students. In short, they are more interested in
the woods than in the trees.

Considerations of speed and efficiency begin to lose their relevance when considered
from the teacher's global perspective. Naturally he wants his students to move along as
rapidly as possible, but overall progress is
more important than the speed at which it
occurs. Clearly, he does not like to waste his
professional energy, but how can he tell
when it is being wasted? What if that half-
hour of private tutoring failed to drive home
the intricacies of long division for Billy but,

instead, did demonstrate to him that his
teacher was vitally concerned with his lack
of progress? Was that time wasted? Most
teachers, I believe, would say, "Of course
not." Even if nothing were accomplished
during that half hour of contact with Billy,
few teachers would mourn the loss of their
time and energy. Sometimes things work and
sometimes they do not. The teacher who is
immersed in his work has more important
worries than smoothness and efficiency. Consequently, he is not very sensitive to charges
of sloppiness and inefficiency, for his own es-
timates of his ability are more closely tied to
other aspects of his functioning. The claims
of more haste and less waste made for many
of the technological advances, therefore, are
only mildly interesting to him.

Although teachers' attitudes can act as
deterrents to change, their lukewarm enthusi-
asm and even their overt hostility toward a
specific technique might be overcome if it
could be demonstrated that the technique in
in question were unequivocally superior
in achieving specific educational goals. If
Johnny could really read after a few sessions

with an electronic typewriter, the heel-dragging efforts of teachers would probably not be an insurmountable obstacle to the rapid adoption of the device. But the demonstration of effectiveness in educational affairs is a difficult task and the establishment of the relative superiority of one method of teaching over another is even more so.

It is perhaps inevitable that each time a new instructional method is developed, attempts are made to establish its relative effectiveness as compared with earlier methods. But, more often than not, the results of such comparisons turn out to be disappointingly ambiguous. Faced with this situation, one leader in the field of auto-instructional devices, Professor L. M. Stolurow, has called for a complete halt to comparative studies. He states,

One feature of research on auto-instruction I hope will not be with us in the future is the comparative study. Currently in auto-instructional research there is blind repetition, if not stubborn persistence in the use of the comparative methods of research design. Film and TV research has shown this same pattern. Interestingly, this type of study is inappropriate when we know very little about a complex phenomenon; yet it seems to be at its peak in its compelling quality at the very time it is least likely to be useful. . . . If we know anything, we know that a comparative study cannot produce generalizable results. . . . My prediction and firm hope is that the comparative study in which a teaching machine program is compared with live teaching will become extinct.[5]

Not only are comparative studies tremendously complex; they also commonly fail to consider two important contingencies that may be associated with one or both of the methods being compared. The first is that the new method may involve not only a change in the way of reaching old goals, but a change in goals as well. Take as an instance, the recent interest in so-called "discovery methods" for teaching science. Advocates of this approach desire not only that new methods of teaching be used, but that new results be sought also. For them, the question of whether the student has learned a set of scientific facts is less important than whether he has learned to construct hypotheses, to weigh evidence, and the like. Ob-

5. L. M. Stolurow, *op. cit.*, p. 520–21.

viously, it makes little sense to compare this new procedure with the old by using conventional tests of school achievement. In fact, there are few if any sensible ways of making an empirically sound comparison between these two instructional programs. A similar situation exists with respect to many other proposed innovations. Often the important question is not whether the new method is better than the old but, rather, whether the new method accomplishes the specific ends for which it was designed.

A second complication in many comparison studies is the possibility of unexamined side effects. In his zest to establish the relative superiority of one method over another, the proponent of a new technique often fails to be on the lookout for these tangential, yet potentially significant, effects. There is some indication that research on the newer educational media has been particularly neglectful in this regard. One pair of sociologists, focusing on studies of educational television, comment as follows:

We need answers to questions about the long term consequences, such as the impact on student interests, morale, values, and on student social organization, aspects which lie outside the conventional experimental format. Rarely (if ever) is the crucial question asked: What is the impact of television instruction upon the teaching staff, the student body, and the whole organizational capacity of the educational institution? What are the effects on socialization of television instruction? In short: What are the side effects—when the side effects may be more powerful than the direct effects?[6]

Lacking compelling evidence of the superiority of some of the newer educational devices, educators, particularly school administrators and members of school boards, are apt to move cautiously. This does not mean that adoptions will not be made, for though it is hard to demonstrate the advantages of the new it is also true that most of the current practices in our schools are equally lacking in the kind of empirical support that might insure their continuance. But when changes are made they are more likely to be supported by rhetoric and by the profes-

6. Morris Janowitz and David Street, "The social organization of education," in *The New Media and Education: Their Impact on Society*, ed. Peter H. Rossi and Bruce J. Biddle, Chicago: Aldine, 1966, p. 211.

sional prestige of their advocates than by an appeal to concrete empirical data.

One result of this state of affairs, which has profound implications for the future work of teachers, is the cyclic parade of fads and fashions that drift across the educational scene. Lacking a clear criterion of effectiveness, educators, from state superintendents to classroom teachers, are inclined to keep an eye out for the latest trend in educational opinion. Newsletters, speakers at conventions, and professional consultants pass the word on to local school systems. In-service workshops, clinics, and institutes are established to keep teachers up-to-date in their practices. A few years ago the focus was on the gifted child; then came a wave of interest in creativity; more recently, the topic of cultural deprivation has held the center of the educational stage. Underlying these broad changes in focus, one can detect contrapuntal shifts of interest in specific teaching practices and curricular topics—i.t.a., the new math, sex education, the dropout problem—each has created a flurry of excitement followed by a period of reappraisal and relative calm.

This description of changing interests is not meant to imply that nothing endures in the classroom. Fashions come and go but styles remain, and even the most shortlived fad probably leaves its mark on future practice. The point is that these fluctuations of opinion, which have been going on for some time and will probably continue to do so, have a thwarting effect on efforts to produce massive and enduring changes within the schools.

In the absence of decisive evidence on which to base change, and confronted by competing appeals for their attention and loyalty, educators are apt to seem fickle to the serious proponent of the latest innovation. And this fickleness has some justification, for teachers have learned from experience that today's educational advice is apt to vanish as quickly and as mysteriously as last year's television programs. In short, whether we like it or not, the dynamics of educational innovation more closely resemble the tides of change within the garment industry than they do the path of progress within the medical profession. Educational technologists may deplore this state of affairs, but they are not likely to change it significantly.

Given the pressures from government and industry urging educators to experiment with newer technological devices, it is almost inevitable that their use will become more widespread. But widespread adoption does not necessarily mean penetration into a significant number of classrooms. Under the conditions that have been described, there is likely to occur what Janowitz and Street have termed "token saturation," by which they mean "the existence of wide availability of mechanical devices but their extensive underutilization and compartmentalization from the main body of the educational experience of the students."[7]

If the unit of analysis is a school district or a school building, the figures depicting the adoption of these newer devices are indeed impressive. An illustrative set of these figures is presented in the table below.

But the amount of classroom penetration rep-

7. *Ibid.,* p. 225.

Percentage of Principals Reporting the Use Their Schools
Have Made or Will Make of the Media Listed*

Media	1955–56	1960–61	1965–66 (Expectation)
Films and filmstrips			
Elementary.......	88%	96%	99%
Secondary.........	96	99	99
Language labs			
Elementary........	27	36	74
Secondary.........	6	35	83
Tape recorders			
Elementary........	54	74	93
Secondary.........	76	96	99
Teaching Machines			
Elementary........	22	26	71
Secondary.........	5	13	65
TV programs			
Elementary........	25	53	84
Secondary.........	18	51	86

* Adapted from Janowitz and Street, *op. cit.*, p. 225.
The published version does not include figures for elementary principals.

resented by the figures in the table is another matter indeed. The statistics for tape recorders provide a good example of the phenomenon of "token saturation." In 1961, three-fourths of the elementary school principals and almost all of the high school principals reported that their school made some use of a tape recorder. Yet the estimated

number of tape recorders in use in our public schools in that year was 88,000. When divided by the number of operating school
districts in this country (approximately
31,000) the figures on tape recorder use reveal an average of less than 3 units per school
district.[8] Although no figures are available on
the actual use of these scattered units, their
small number would seem to indicate that
they are used rarely by most teachers. Thus,
principals can indeed point with pride to the
modern facilities at work in their schools, but
often they are referring to an insignificant
number of machines, many of which are
probably gathering dust in the audio-visual
aids closet.

The adoption of technological devices in
the schools will undoubtedly increase in the
years ahead, but the word *revolution* is probably inappropriate as a shorthand description of the changes likely to occur. In sum-
mary, the inflexibility of many of these
devices, the attitudinal biases of classroom

8. The statistics on the use of tape recorders are
taken from Henry F. McCusker, Jr. and Philip H. Sor-
enson, "The economics of education," in Rossi and
Biddle, *op. cit.*, p. 187.

teachers, and the lack of clear evidence of instructional effectiveness, are among the forces that could well soften the impact of the new educational technology.

II

Although the advancement of educational technology has its threatening aspects, it also has a certain attractiveness to anyone interested in the improvement of education. The major appeal of technology, particularly among educators, resides in its promise of helping to achieve three conditions that seem to be almost universally desired. These are: (1) the individualization of instruction; (2) the reduction of humdrum and routine activities connected with teaching; and (3) the exposure of all students to top quality instruction and first-rate materials. These three desirables, either singly or in combination, have figured prominently in the arguments presented for the promotion and adoption of almost all forms of educational technology, from the lowly audio-visual aid to the lordly computer console. No conscientious educator can afford to turn a deaf ear to such appeals.

Accordingly, it is appropriate to look more closely at each of these desirable states of affairs with an eye to understanding whether they have the same meaning for educators and technologists alike and whether they represent unalloyed goods that ought to be purchased at almost any cost.

The individualization of instruction, as embodied in a tutorial system, has been an educational ideal for centuries. Indeed, the tutorial arrangement of a one-to-one ratio between teachers and students is described in our earliest accounts of teaching and continues to exist in many parts of the world today. During this century, in particular, there have been countless efforts to modify group instruction in such a way as to make it resemble more closely the ideal pairing of one teacher to one student.

Providing each student with his own tutor, or with an exclusive portion of his teacher's time, however, will not necessarily achieve the goal of individualization. The essential requirement is not that the teacher be alone with his student, but that he respond to the student's uniqueness with pedagogical wisdom. The condition of not having other students present merely increases the likelihood that the teacher will treat the student as an individual; it certainly does not guarantee it. A teacher who is blind to the subtleties of his student's behavior, and who has a narrow repertoire of pedagogical alternatives on which to draw, cannot possibly individualize instruction in anything more than a superficial sense, no matter how many hours he spends alone with his charge.

Several of the educational benefits assumed to accompany the individualization of instruction concern what might be called the economics of learning. They deal principally with the speed and efficiency with which the student masters the material to be learned. These benefits are among those most frequently mentioned when the case for individualization is under discussion. Though interrelated, they can be grouped roughly into three broad classes:

The first has to do with the rate of learning. In an individualized setting, the learner supposedly can move along at a pace that is comfortable to him. He need not wait for his slower peers to catch up, nor must he struggle to keep abreast of his intellectual superiors. The speed with which other learners progress is simply an irrelevant consideration when there are none to serve for comparison.

A second class of alleged benefits focuses on the goodness of fit between the learner and the curriculum. In an individualized setting, the student apparently is presented with learning tasks that are uniquely appropriate to his level of proficiency and that take into account his special strengths and weaknesses. Moreover, the introduction of new tasks is solely dependent on the student's mastery of the old. On the one hand, he will be prevented from wasting time by continuing with a topic or a skill after he has mastered it, and on the other hand, he will not be forced to leave an activity before mastery has been achieved.

A third set of benefits has to do with the continuous monitoring of the student's progress. With a teacher in almost constant attendance, the student will not be allowed to persist in errors, and thus he will avoid learning things that only have to be unlearned at some later date. At the same time, he will be afforded a prompt and continuing appraisal of his educational growth.

Although these seem to be among the most frequently mentioned reasons for seeking the individualization of instruction, they are by no means the only arguments that could be made in its favor. In addition to the benefits that focus on the economics of learning there are those that concern what might be called the dynamics of instruction. These have less to do with questions of speed and efficiency than with the quality of the learning experience and the attitudes engendered by it. Again, it is difficult to discuss these advantages singly, for they are all interrelated, but they too can be classified into three major types.

First are those conditions affecting the psychological distance between the learner, his materials, and his instructor. In the individualized setting, there is commonly a greater intimacy between teacher and student than is true under other circumstances.

This intimacy is achieved in part by greater physical proximity (in tutorial sessions the teacher tends to speak in softer tones and often sits beside the learner rather than standing in front of him), but it is enhanced by other conditions as well. Not only is the teacher closer to the learner in a physical sense, he also is likely to reveal more of his personal life to the learner, and vice versa. (It is worth nothing that tutoring is often done in the home of the teacher or the student, rather than in an "outside" institution.) The result is a greater psychological proximity than that which obtains when the teacher is working with a large group of students. Even the learning materials, to the extent that they are tailored to fit the student, are "his" in a more profound sense than when he is working in a collective setting.

Closely related to the reduction of psychological distance in the learning situation is the degree of importance that comes to be attached to the experience itself. The enhancement of this importance comprises a second class of benefits associated with the dynamics of individualized instruction. An

activity requiring the full attention of a
knowledgeable person is likely to be per-
ceived as more important than one requiring
only his divided attention. If a teacher
spends a large amount of time with one student, his actions not only contain an implicit
evaluation of the activity itself, they also reflect on the worth of the individual with
whom he is working. Thus, when instruction
is individualized, conditions are established
in which it is possible for the student to learn
not only that the process of instruction is
very important but also that he, the learner,
is worthy of personalized attention. Whether
or not this message actually gets across is another matter entirely.

A third type of benefit associated with the
dynamics of instruction and likely enhanced
by individualization has to do with the communication of feeling between the teacher
and his student. When the teacher is in constant attendance he is available not only to
call attention to errors and to affirm correct
responses, but also to beam with pleasure
and to frown with disappointment. In short,
he is on hand to communicate his concern as

well as to instruct. The teacher's involvement and his emotional entanglement with his students can also flourish in a crowded classroom, but he is probably freer to "let himself go" in an affective sense when the student in question is the sole object of his concern.

Here, then, is an overview of the chief advantages of individualized instruction. Although the benefits most frequently mentioned are those having to do with the speed and efficiency of learning, they are clearly not the only reasons that make this situation a desirable one. When instruction is individualized it is also, in an important sense, personalized. As this happens, the student comes to know and to be known by a mature adult who demonstrates, by action and by thought, his personal concern for the student's progress. The communication of this concern may be more important, in the long run, than the more obvious benefits on which educators have focused their attention.

When the complexities of individualized instruction are revealed even to this limited extent, the potential of technical advances for achieving this end is brought into serious question. This is not to say that machines can be of no help in the process. But they are clearly not the only answer to the problem, as is suggested by some critics. In fact, the aspects of individualization that might make the fullest use of the machine's power —such as the goals of varying learning rates and providing constant feedback—are precisely the ones about which there seems to be the greatest need for further discussion and debate.

It has been reported that with the aid of a computerized tutorial system the brightest child in a class may move along at a rate five or ten times faster than that of the slowest child in the room. This statement may be startling to persons unacquainted with classroom affairs, but as most experienced teachers know, differences as large as that are a commonplace in today's schools. Even without the aid of a computer it is not at all unusual to have some students finish in ten minutes an assignment that it takes others an hour to complete; every teacher knows that some students will read ten pages in the time it takes others to read one.

Unfortunately, the educational problem created by these differences in ability is not solved simply by creating conditions under which each student may move along at his own rate. A recognition of variability in learning speed does not tell us what to do about it. If Billy can complete in five minutes an arithmetic assignment that takes Sammy fifty minutes to complete, should Billy spend an additional forty-five minutes on arithmetic, thus moving far ahead of Sammy? Perhaps he should, but then again, maybe not. It may well be that Billy would be better off spending his "extra" time on his language arts workbook, or finishing his science project, or casually browsing through the books on the library shelf. Perhaps by breezing through his arithmetic lesson in five minutes Billy is also learning that arithmetic is "a snap," whereas another forty-five minutes would convince him otherwise. As the problem is posed no one knows for sure what to do with Billy, except perhaps the teacher who works with him daily, and even he must have his doubts. The point is that individualization of instruction involves much more than clearing the educational path of obstacles so that students may hobble or dash along as fast as their intellectual legs can carry them.

In point of fact, the greatest barrier to coping with differences in individual learning rates is the graded school system, not the human teacher. Miss Jones, with little effort, could move some of her third graders along to fifth grade mathematics but the tradition of not overstepping her legally defined boundaries, coupled with the practices of textbook packaging, prevent her from easily doing so. Machines alone will not solve this problem, although their mass adoption could well bring the issue to a head.

The goal of fitting learning materials to the unique characteristics of the student entails another set of practices requiring serious scrutiny before we conclude that the machine can do the job better than humans. As it is commonly discussed, the concept of an ideal match between the learner and his materials or between the learner and an instruc-

tional methodology is probably as romantic
and as unrealistic a notion as the concept of
an ideal marriage. Just as all marriages, outside of storybooks, involve compromise and
adjustment, so too, in a more trivial sense
perhaps, do all learning encounters. The
teacher, or the machine, may hope to locate
just the right exercise or the perfect example
for Billy at a given moment of instruction,
but chances are they will miss the mark by at
least a little bit. Happily, the miss will probably not matter very much insofar as Billy's
learning is concerned. Even with an approxi-
mate fit, Billy seems to make do and appears
to benefit from the experience. The marriage
between the learner and his materials can
surely benefit from some behind-the-scenes
maneuvering, but as an educational match-
maker it is doubtful that the machine's ca-
pacities are significantly greater than those
of the teacher.

The advantages of having the machine in
constant attendance to monitor the student's
successes and failures is another topic about
which there is room for further discussion. At
first glance, it would seem beneficial to have

errors and misunderstandings corrected immediately. If a pupil adds five and three and
gets nine, or reads "was" for "saw," surely he
will be better off if the teacher informs him
of his mistake as soon as it happens. But the
validity of this assumption is not as great as
it might appear. Consider, as an instance, the
pre-school child who is pretending to read or
who is just learning how to count. Is it better,
pedagogically, to correct his many errors as
they occur, or should we applaud his efforts
while smiling inwardly at his naïveté? The
experimental evidence may be unclear on
this point, but the intuitive wisdom of generations of parents is almost unanimous and
cannot be lightly brushed aside.

There is certainly much that we do not
know about how to inform a student of his
progress, but most teachers would probably
agree that there are times when it is unwise
to tell a student he is wrong, even if he is. At
times it may be better to allow a student to
think he can do something even when we
know he cannot. Perhaps a belief in one's
powers precedes their realization.

Even if it were possible, therefore, to monitor each and every student's response and to provide instant feedback on the current status of educational growth, there is at least some question about whether we should hasten to provide such a service. Even if it were shown that students would learn more rapidly under conditions of constant surveillance, the issue would not be settled, for it would still be necessary to show that no attitudinal damage had been done.

The line between simply informing a person of his weaknesses and nagging him about them is sometimes easily crossed. Among the conditions that increase the likelihood of crossing this boundary are the frequency and consistency with which errors are pointed out. A nagging housewife may succeed in having her husband walk the straight and narrow if she keeps after him enough, but her success is often accomplished at some risk to the stability of her marriage. Even after a few hours of human surveillance most students are glad to get out for an afternoon. If machines greatly increased the frequency of watchfulness and prodding in the classroom, the desire to escape might be even greater. We must certainly be cautious about doing anything that could inflate the educational divorce rate.

When it comes to the personalization of learning—as contrasted with the individualization of such things as learning rate, materials, and feedback—machines, even those that only exist in the dreams of inventors, do not begin to compete with the human teacher. The reason for this lack of competition is simply that a machine is not a person. It is embarrassing to have to state the obvious, but unfortunately, this basic fact often seems to get lost in the shuffle in discussions of the potential of the machine in the classroom. Although a computer can store almost countless pieces of information about a student, it cannot *know* him as one person knows another. Moreover, it cannot *know* the subject a student is studying, even though its memory cells are packed to capacity. A machine may be able to dispense praise and reproof according to the most complicated set of instructions—it may even, when so doing, exude the mellifluous tones of an Everett Dirksen—but this marvelous performance should not allow us to overlook the fact that the machine cannot begin to *care* whether the student learns anything or not. Only humans care about humans, machines never do. Thus, what is here being called the personalization of instruction lies completely outside of the machine's capacity. The most elaborate computer ever developed will never know a student in the same sense as does the bus driver who takes him home in the afternoon, nor will it ever care more about his progress than does the janitor who shuffles past him in the hall.

This fundamental incapacity of the machine deserves further comment. As our technology develops, so too does our ability to produce machines with a greater number of humanoid features. Computer experts talk optimistically about the time, in the not-too-distant future, when machines will converse with students, reason with them, and presumably even emit a kindly chuckle or two when their electronic scanners brush over a harmless mistake. These added touches of realism are indeed impressive as feats of engineering, but they do not significantly reduce the gap between the human and the non-human. From the standpoint of personalizing the learning encounter, the advantages of lifelike mechanical instructors are dubious indeed. Some understanding of why this is so can be gained by considering the difference between playthings and real things.

In recent years, toy manufacturers have gone out of their way to produce objects that stimulate reality. Dolls that *really* cry, trucks that *really* roar, irons that *really* get hot, and other just-like-the-real-thing contraptions crowd the shelves of our toy departments. Many children seem to like these simulated wonders, or at least their parents do, for thousands of them are purchased each year. Yet children, as they mature, begin to grow tired of the artificial and increasingly insist on dealing with genuine objects rather than toys. This gradual rejection of the artificial has little to do with the toy's superficial realism or lack of it. Toy manufacturers cannot keep teenage girls in the dolls' corner by adding salt to the doll's tears or by producing a Raggedy Ann who speaks in complex sentences. Even a locomotive belching real smoke will not keep a gang of adolescent boys on their hands and knees for very long. This is so because the child's separation from his toys is brought on not by any disappointment with the facsimile as such, but by his increasing need to distinguish sharply between fantasy and reality. Gradually he comes to realize that toys remain toys no matter how realistic they might become. No manner of magic, except the pre-logical rationality of the young child, can bridge the gap between the plastic truck on the living room floor and the real McCoy rumbling by on the street outside.

The same tendency that leads to the ultimate rejection of make-believe will likely have some effect on the student's willingness to "converse" and "reason" with a computer console. Engineers can add sound, color, canned applause, and even low-heeled oxfords, but their product will forever remain a toy teacher, not a real one. This does not mean that the machine is unable to perform instructional tasks; we have long known that even the crudest toy can have educational value. But young people have a way of casting toys aside long before they have learned all they might from them. All things considered, this is a sign of health and we must be quite as willing to applaud it in the classroom as we do on the playground.

Although we typically associate individualized instruction with the achievement of a one-to-one teacher/pupil ratio, there is no reason why a considerable amount of individualization cannot go on while the teacher is working with a group of students. As he responds to a student's query during class discussion, as he pauses to clear up another student's misunderstanding, even as he snaps his fingers to bring the inattentive daydreamer back into the center of things, the teacher is achieving a degree of individualization even though thirty pairs of eyes happen to be on him. When the richness of the teacher's knowledge of individual students and the complexity of his pedagogical moves, even in a crowded classroom, are compared with those of any of the machines now available, it is easy to see why many teachers are inclined to be suspicious of the

programmer's use of the term "individualized instruction."

A second claim frequently put forward by
promoters of educational technology has to
do with eliminating many of the humdrum
and routine activities connected with teaching. The possibility of freeing the teacher
from routine tasks is an especially attractive
argument because of the many hours teachers spend performing clerical duties. But this
possibility, though often advanced as one of
the arguments in favor of programmed instruction, is by no means a guaranteed outcome of the teaching machine movement. In
fact, some authorities think that the teacher
might become more, rather than less, bur-
dened by clerical work if certain types of
machines take over a large part of the instructional job. Stolurow, for example, paints
a disturbing picture of the teacher's duties in
connection with conventional teaching machines.

The smaller machines need to be loaded and un-
loaded. They have to be set up for every new
student, each period of the day. Every student
has to be relocated in his program at the point

where he left off. This means that after the program is inserted, the place must be found and the recording tape reset. The teacher who does this for 25 to 50 students every 35 to 50 minutes will find some way to escape from the situation. Even figuring one minute per student, a conservative estimate, these activities would add up to 30 to 40 minutes per period per teacher in simple mechanical work.

If the machine uses a program printed in paper scroll, rather than on separate sheets, then someone has to make up the scroll. Usually this means attaching the separate pages together after mimeographing them, and rolling them up for use. Once used they need to be unrolled. Each scroll has to be individually handled to locate every student in the place where he left off at the last period.

If teachers are to grade the students, they will have to examine the students' response records to decide about the students' progress. The other alternative is to give tests at the end of each program unit. This latter procedure means that for each student at every period of the school day, the teacher will have from 40 to 150 items per student to check before the next day. Also, if the time taken by the student is considered, then this is another datum to be processed each day. Put it all together, and it becomes a big job. Research workers don't mind doing these things. In fact, they are used to it, however, even they do not do it daily, year in and year out. Not many of today's teachers will do it.[9]

Stolurow's proposed solution to this problem is to present programmed material in a book format or to employ computer-based teaching machines systems. These alternatives would relieve the teacher from the business of loading and unloading machines and possibly also from the detailed grading of individual items. But the amount of routine required even under these conditions remains an open question.

If we are in earnest about trying to free teachers from some of the clerical duties that now assail them, there are several other possibilities that ought to be explored, in addition to those involving mechanical assistance. One alternative would be to assign a part-time assistant to every teacher who wanted one. These assistants, who probably need have no more than a high school education, could be recruited from among the housewives in the local community or they could

9. Stolurow, *op. cit.*, p. 523.

include persons preparing to teach. The cost
of such help would not be prohibitive. If an
assistant were employed for ten hours a week
at two dollars an hour, the total cost for the
academic year would be about eight hun-
dred dollars, which comes to about one-
eighth of a full time teacher's salary. This
price may seem high, but it surely is no
higher than the cost connected with many of
the mechanical aids now under consideration. In addition, the use of assistants has the
advantage of contributing to the professional
status of the teacher, an outcome that could
be of inestimable benefit in helping to recruit
larger numbers of able people to the field.

In the view of a few of its most enthusiastic supporters, the machine promises to do
much more than relieve teachers of some of
the pedestrian and trivial aspects of their
work. Instead, these enthusiasts claim, it will
ultimately take over the major burden of instruction in several of the core school subjects. If this prediction comes true it will
create an additional problem, for the teacher
will then be faced not just with free time on
his hands, but with a markedly different set

of professional expectations. Professor Patrick Suppes, one of the foremost proponents of computer-assisted instruction, minces no words in his description of things to come. "It will be evident that well-structured subjects such as reading and mathematics can easily be handled by tutorial systems to carry the main load of teaching such subjects. . . . It will remain the teacher's responsibility to attempt the challenging task of helping students who are not proceeding successfully with the tutorial program and who need special attention."[10]

Suppes' brief reference to the teacher's task in the age of the computer, a task which would seem to consist chiefly of helping to salvage the machine's failures, is clearly very different from our present definition of the teacher's role. Such a new set of expectations may indeed be challenging, but certainly no more so than the duties the teacher now performs. Moreover, if he is to become a remedial specialist in the core school subjects, the teacher will no doubt have to give up

10. P. Suppes, "The uses of computers in education," *Scientific American*, 215: 218–19 (September 1966).

some of the professional rewards he currently enjoys. For example, the pleasure of contributing to the development of the ablest students is, for many teachers, as satisfying as that derived from helping those who are having special problems. Yet this experience, it would seem, will remain for the machine alone to enjoy. Naturally, if the computer or any other device could greatly improve the quality of instruction, the price of depriving teachers of a few of their old-fashioned pleasures would not be too great. But, as we have seen, the relative superiority of mechanized instruction is yet to be demonstrated and even if it had been we would still be obliged to weigh all of the losses that such a change might entail.

The teacher's daily work is not the only aspect of his role that could be affected by the changes being discussed here. His status might be altered as well. At present, the social position of teachers in our society is relatively low when compared with other professional groups. In fact, some people think that the very word "professional" is inappropriately applied to teachers. Yet the teacher's influence on his students, his ability to command their respect and to have them do the things he believes will benefit them, are in no small measure affected by the status attached to his role.

A few advocates of change argue that the newer technological advances will serve to enhance the status of the teacher by helping to place his work on a solid scientific foundation. But the promise of transforming pedagogy into a science has been made before, and, regrettably, the professionals who have gained most from efforts in that direction have been educational researchers, not teachers. If the teacher's contribution to the achievement of instructional goals is diminished or if he comes to be looked upon as the servant to a new breed of "educational scientists," or a third string substitute for the "real" professional who performs the televised lecture, the effect on his classroom influence and on his general morale could be detrimental. Again we are faced with the difficulty of not really knowing what might occur if some of the predicted technological

changes come into being. Lacking this
knowledge, we must be sufficiently prudent
to envision the worst that could happen, as
well as the best.

Perhaps the most attractive of all the appeals associated with educational technology are those having to do with upgrading
the quality of instruction through the im-
proved organization of materials, flawlessly
displayed. In the case of programmed instruction this goal is expected to be realized
through the detailed analysis of curricular
content and a clear delineation of the steps
by which mastery is achieved. Other forms
of technology, such as educational television
and instructional films, promise to make
available the services of master teachers at
the flick of a switch. A good example of the
height of these expectations is contained in
Professor Suppes' introduction to an article
on computer-assisted instruction. As Suppes
sees it, "One can predict that in a few more
years millions of school children will have
access to what Philip of Macedon's son,
Alexander, enjoyed as a royal prerogative:

the personal services of a tutor as well-informed and responsive as Aristotle."[11]

Before taking Professor Suppes' prediction seriously, it is tempting to have some fun with it. Here, indeed, is an image to warm the cockles of every middle-class parent's heart! Imagine one's own little Johnny sitting beside an ersatz Aristotle—like a royal prince! Who needs old fuddy-duddy Miss Jones when the grand old Greek himself, or a reasonable facsimile thereof, can be installed in every classroom? Why not encourage our school boards to hurry out to their nearest technician and put their orders in immediately? A ready answer, of course, is that these promises are still only glints in the technicians' eyes and are likely to remain so for some time to come. But there are more profound reasons for looking before we leap.

We might begin by taking the example quite literally (perhaps too literally) and asking whether Aristotle himself, were he alive, would be a better teacher of first-grade reading or of third-grade arithmetic than would poor old Miss Jones, armed only with

11. Suppes, *op. cit.*, p. 207.

a copy of Dick and Jane and a stack of SMSG
workbooks. At first glance, the comparison
seems ridiculous. Surely the old sage would
run rings around any of the local competition. But why should he? Because his thinking is more logical? Because he has more
facts at his fingertips? Because he has a
higher IQ? We have already examined differences in these qualities among living
teachers and have found them to be only
slightly related to conventional measures of
student progress. Apparently the more Aris-
totle-like members of our teaching profession
do not do a significantly better job of teaching the tool subjects to young children than
their less gifted colleagues.

Unfortunately, most studies of the effect of
intellectual ability on teaching performance
have looked at teachers working in regular
classrooms. Perhaps differences in ability
would have a greater impact in tutorial set-
tings than they have in rooms full of thirty or
more students. Also, the gap between Aristotle and ordinary mortals is allegedly much
greater than is the range of abilities to be
found within a normal population of teach-

ers. Perhaps a teacher with an IQ of 150 cannot teach reading much better than his more modestly endowed colleagues, but what if he were truly as omniscient as Aristotle? Because no one knows the answer to these questions the argument moves from the merely fanciful to the ridiculous and ought to be abandoned. Nonetheless, we should remember that Aristotle's fame does not rest on his ability to teach the three R's to a grade school child. Possibly he would have done the job magnificently, possibly not. For all we know, Philip of Macedon's son might have required special tutoring from a middle-aged spinster on the side.

Taking the analogy between Aristotle and the computer more in the spirit in which it was intended, we might inquire into the problems of constructing sagacious machines that would respond in an Aristotelian manner to the young learner's attempts at mastering reading or arithmetic. Such an inquiry is far from fanciful, for experimental models of devices designed to do just that are already in operation in several schools.

As we think about the kind of knowledge

necessary to build such a machine, the limits of our pedagogical know-how are quickly revealed. The machine, we must remember, will do only what we tell it to do, and nothing more. We must decide under what conditions the machine should reward students and when it should not. We must decide whether bright students should work on the same material as do their duller classmates. We must decide when to introduce phonics into the reading lesson. We must decide what to do about students' errors, unanticipated responses, and lapses of memory. The sorry truth, of course, is that even our wisest teachers do not know the answers to these pedagogical questions, or at least they do not know them well enough to allow their translation into machine language.

In the eyes of some, however, the answers to these perplexing questions are just around the corner. They claim that the solutions will be found in short order, especially if we use the machine to help in the search. This belief rests on the assumption that there are answers to most of the "ought" questions of pedagogy. All that is required to find them is the proper empirical technique. But such assumptions seem to spring from an incomplete understanding of what teaching is all about.

In a way, the business of deciding in advance exactly how to teach is like asking a baseball pitcher to predict precisely what kind of a pitch will elicit a strike from the batter. True, he can make an educated guess based on his prior knowledge of the batter's habits, his stance at the plate, the position of the runners on base, the signals sent by the catcher, and the like—but a guess it remains. He has no choice, therefore, but to try what he thinks will work and to hope for the best. The teacher's position is analogous, except that his task and the contingencies operating to affect it are infinitely more complex. He too is forced to use guesswork much of the time. On some days he is lucky and on others he is not. But when the teacher is asked to explain his successes and failures he, like the pitcher, is often unable to put his finger on the exact combination of circumstances that accounted for them. More important, it would probably not do him much good to

try, for those particular constellations of
events will never recur. The same teaching
procedure tried twice will never have exactly
the same effect.

It is unlikely that the machine can improve
appreciably on the teacher's guesswork, operating, as it must, on merely a partial translation of a teacher's skill. As we learn more
about the process of education, the teacher's
guesses, and therefore those of the machine,
are bound to improve. But tons of empirical
knowledge are unlikely to eliminate the necessary element of artistry lying at the heart
of the teacher's work.

In the final analysis, the miracle of the
machine's achievement is not miraculous at
all, except for the fact that it is accomplished
by a machine rather than by a human. We
applaud its work as we applaud a dancing
elephant, not because the performance is
outstanding, but because it has the audacity
to try.

III

Critical discussions of machines and their
impact on society customarily end on an

ominous note. Such gloomy finales usually
make it quite clear, if there is any doubt left
by then, that the machine is the villain in
whose clutches man cannot but suffer a vex-
atious future. This conclusion is often pre-
ceded by some mention of the process of de-
humanization and the casual role played in
that process by the machine. What is often
missing in these dire forecasts is the realization that it is not the machine itself but the
ideological climate underlying its misuse
that creates the real danger. Furthermore,
we sometimes overlook the fact that a world
view condoning the abuse of man by machines and by other methods as well does
not depend on the existence of machines for
its emergence. Although technology, when
improperly employed, may exacerbate human discomfort, it is by no means essential.
Man is quite capable of treating his fellow
man inhumanly without the aid of pul-
leys and gears. He has been doing so for
centuries.

In his recent book, *The Myth of the Machine*,[12] Lewis Mumford provides a disturb-

12. Harcourt, Brace & World, 1967.

ing account of the evolution, early in human history, of forms of social organization and control by which hundreds of thousands of people were condemned to a level of sub-human existence as members of highly co-ordinated labor forces serving their king. These armies of workers, which Mumford calls "megamachines," did manage to erect architectural wonders, such as the great pyramids in Egypt, but the cost in human terms was awesome.

Mumford's historical analysis offers ample documentation of our general thesis: the gravest threat to man's well-being, now as in generations past, is not the machine qua machine but those persons and institutions that applaud and support a mechanistic approach to human affairs. From this it follows that the greatest intellectual challenge of our time is not how to design machines that behave more and more like humans, but rather, how to protect humans from being treated more and more like machines.

American educators, looking back on the changes that have taken place in our schools during the past century, are apt to be complacent, if not smug, about the status of the modern classroom as a humanizing environment. To anyone who recalls the past, our schools obviously are better today than ever before. No longer do students sit in fixed rows, their hands folded in front of them and their eyes front. Gone is the hickory stick and the petty tyrant who wielded it. If reading, writing, and arithmetic are taught to the tune of anything these days, it is the soft hum of the air conditioner in the back of the room. In slang parlance, students never had it so good.

Our educators are undoubtedly justified in pointing with pride to these improvements. Only the most cynical critic could fail to applaud their efforts. Yet, as our studies of Organization Man have clearly shown, human life can be stripped of dignity and meaning by methods that are subtle and unpremeditated as well as by those that are blatant and open in their intent. No one sets out to turn the factory worker into an insensate blob or the company salesman into a fatuous handshaker, but, somehow, many wind up that way. It is not fair to place all

the blame for these unhappy creations on ge-
netic determinants or on early childhood experiences. Propensities toward these and
other stunted conditions may develop early
in life, but they require continual support
and confirmation before they harden into a
style of living.

As we think about some of the more in-
conspicuous ways in which the school experience might inadvertently contribute to a
student's loss of self-esteem and personal
worth, the picture is not quite as rosy as the
fact of the movable chairs and a smiling
teacher would have us believe. In discussing
these less rosy aspects of classroom life, my
intention is not to alarm, nor to create the
impression that school is hell. We know that
many, possibly most, students come to school
gladly and expectantly, though we must also
admit that many do not. My purpose is simply to call attention to a few of the features
of classroom life about which we may not
have given enough thought and which may
be having an undesirable cumulative effect
on many students.

In human terms, mechanization refers to

the process by which people are treated mechanically; that is, without giving thought to what is going on inside them. The willful operation of this process also implies a set of beliefs concerning the importance of such abstract qualities as freedom, responsibility, and choice. These more profound aspects of the topic will be ignored in the following discussion, although the discerning reader will easily detect the points at which a deeper analysis of the issues is warranted. For the most part, I shall try to keep my remarks at a practical level, looking at the things we see and do when students are before us. Before moving into the classroom, however, it is necessary to describe the type of phenomena we are looking for.

One way of identifying the various ways in which humans might be treated mechanically is to think about how we treat machines and what our attitudes are toward them and then to ask whether there are any interpersonal counterparts to these man-machine confrontations. For example, most machines passively comply with the will of their operators. We turn them on and off whenever it suits our fancy. Thus, to the extent that we turn humans "on" and "off" without giving thought to their desire to be activated or halted, we are in almost a literal sense, behaving toward them as we behave toward machines. This is not to say that such starts and stops are always harmful. Indeed, they may often be beneficial. But regardless of their effect, they contain elements of a mechanistic approach to human affairs.

Not only is it never necessary to ask a machine whether it wants to be on or off, it is equally unnecessary to offer it an explanation of why it is working. Lacking sentience, machines are dutiful servants of their owners, guaranteed never to revolt. The translation of this condition to the human situation is easy enough. When we expect people to do what we say without question, and when we fail to offer an explanation of our commands, we are adopting a stance toward our fellow beings similar to the one with which we confront the machine.

At the heart of the man-machine relationship is the concept of ownership. Machines belong to people: they have no plans of their own and no future extending beyond the period of their servitude. This basic condition is clearly evident among humans in various forms of slavery, but there are many less extreme equivalencies as well. Webster defines a slave as "one who has lost control of himself and his freedom of action." In this broad sense the term appropriately describes a much wider range of social arrangements than those to which common usage limits it. Whenever a person unwillingly relinquishes his own plans and places his energies at the disposal of someone else he is, for that moment at least, a slave.

Another aspect of machine-oriented thought that has its parallel in our thinking about human affairs concerns the meaning of work and related activities. Machines, as we know, are all work and no play. Although we may play with machines, it is we who do the playing, not they. In our daily lives, however, the distinction between these two classes of activity is not always evident. Often we work and play at the same time and it is not possible to say where one ends and the other begins. To the extent that we insist on a sharp division between these two modes of relating to the world and particularly when we then proceed to deprecate playfulness by sharply restricting the opportunities for its emergence, we are creating a set of expectations similar to those we hold for the machine. All work and no play not only made Jack a dull boy, it also made him something less than human.

Idleness is a condition akin to play and one that is also prominent in our thinking about machines. When machines are idle their potential is being wasted. Moreover, idleness, in the language used to talk about machines, simply means not in use. When, in our dealings with humans, we define idleness in these same terms we run the risk of ignoring important internal evidence that might alter our opinion. In other words, people may appear to be idle when they are not. In truth, we can rarely tell when a person is idle simply by looking at him, unless we are thinking of him as a machine. We often can tell whether he is doing what we want him to, but that is quite a different judgment.

An important characteristic of our dealings

with machines involves the practice of judging a machine's worth by the quality of its products. Although we may admire its internal workings, the real value of a machine rests on tangible evidence of work completed. Men, too, are capable of producing things and of leaving their mark on the world. But their worth as humans is only partially determined by the tangible residue of their actions. Furthermore, in the life of a man, as the verse of the old popular ditty reminds us, it often "ain't what he does but the way that he does it" that really counts. When we ignore these qualitative aspects of experience and focus exclusively on end products (sometimes solemnly referred to by researchers as "output variables") we might as well be discussing the performance of a sportscar for all the difference it makes.

Of all the distinctions between our approaches to machines and to humans, the most profound involves our capacity for empathy, for imaginatively projecting our own consciousness into another being. Obviously, it makes no sense to empathize with a machine, for the machine has no consciousness that we might vicariously share. Consequently, it is impossible to feel sorry for a machine, or to envy it, or to be understanding when it fails to function properly. These same responses, however, are not only possible between two persons, they are the basic ingredients of a humane environment. When we stop trying to imagine how the other person feels, or what he is thinking, or how we might behave in a similar situation, we have severed the most vital link binding us to other living creatures.

As we ponder the many ways in which people might be treated like machines, it becomes evident that there probably is no escape from such treatment. All of us, almost every day of our lives, are required to do things we do not want to do and to perform acts whose full meaning eludes us. We all know what it is like to be treated as an impersonal object and to be judged by our products rather than by our intentions and aspirations. For most of us the worlds of work and play are sharply divided and there is far too little time and space for the latter.

The issue turns, therefore, not on the absolute occurrence of these experiences but on their frequency and, more important, on their necessity. These considerations are especially relevant when we think about what goes on in school. Thus, the question is not whether we treat our students in the manner herein described. Of course we do. It is more important to ask how often these things happen and whether the frequency of their occurrence is a matter of necessity or simply the result of our unmindfulness. No teacher I have ever met would admit to setting out deliberately to create a miserable environment for his students. Therefore, if schools do less than they might in allowing their inhabitants to achieve full human stature, their shortcomings must either be inevitable or else they must be caused by our failure to see what is happening.

Recently I had an experience in a classroom that forced me to reflect on these questions more than I previously had. It was not a surprising or dramatic experience. In fact, it was quite ordinary. Yet, strangely enough, its typicality is the very quality that gives importance to what I witnessed and makes it worth relating here. It occurred during a morning visit to a summer school class that had been organized for a group of twenty gifted elementary school students in a Canadian city. The children attending this class had been drawn from several schools spread throughout the system. Each had scored 130 or better on a group intelligence test and all were scheduled to enter the fifth grade in the fall. Recruitment for the class had been accomplished by sending a note home to the parents of each student inviting them to enroll their child in a special summer session for the academically able. A small group of educators who were specially interested in gifted children helped to organize the curriculum, made frequent observations of the class, and met with the classroom teacher each day, after dismissal, to discuss the work of these children and the general topic of giftedness. A university professor was in charge of this seminar and it was he who asked me to visit the class and to meet with his group following the morning session.

On the day of my visit I entered the classroom before school began to find that most of the students had already arrived and were clustered around a table on which were displayed a collection of Oriental musical instruments—drums, chimes, cymbals, and the like. The teacher was not present at the time, presumably having gone on an errand of some kind. While I sat quietly, almost unobserved, in the back of the room, the children around the table began to play with the musical instruments, at first timidly and then with increasing boldness. As the activity progressed the noise increased, until the sound of individual instruments became almost indistinguishable in the general din. A few of the children were obviously competing with each other to see who could produce the loudest noise. Others appeared to be intent on the instrument they were playing and were seemingly oblivious to the noise around them. A few of the students (all girls) had already taken their seats and were watching the group at the table. One girl sat with a book in front of her, her fingers in her ears. At this point the teacher, a pleasant-looking man whom I judged to be in his mid-forties, entered the room. He walked toward the table with his arms extended. "All right, people," he said, "Let's get back to our seats so we can have opening exercises." He looked back at me and smiled apologetically. Without any visible signs of complaint the students stopped playing the instruments and returned to their seats—two boys sprinting to get there. One of the girls who had been seated stepped to the teacher's desk, picked up the Bible, and read one of the Psalms aloud to the class. The Lord's Prayer was recited in unison, with the class standing, the Bible was returned to the teacher's desk, and the students sat again. The school day had begun.

That morning the class was working on a project involving the comparison of life during an earlier historical period with conditions prevalent today. The children had been given their choice of the earlier period to be used in the contrast and they had selected fifth-century Rome. The class had then been divided into small committees, each assigned a particular aspect of Roman life—e.g., clothing, laws, family life—on which to do research. These committees had been assembling materials for several days and now they were preparing to write reports on their topics.

The teacher began the session by addressing the entire class with the question: "What have you been doing in school these past few days?" A few hands went up and the boy who was called on replied that they had been collecting information. "Fine!" said the teacher, as he wrote "Collecting information" on the board, "and what else have we been doing?" Another volunteer (this time a girl) suggested that they had been recording facts. The teacher called this contribution "good" and wrote "Recording facts" on the board. He then went on to ask what they were going to do with the facts now that they were recorded. Three students raised their hands and the one who was called on said the facts would become part of the reports they were preparing. "Good," said the teacher and then, leaning forward with something of a twinkle in his eye, he asked, "Now, when we put our facts in our report will we put them in exactly as we have found them?" A boy's hand shot into the air and when the teacher

nodded at him he promptly answered,
"Yes!" The teacher looked surprised. "Will
we, Billy? Will we put the facts in our reports
exactly as we found them? If I wanted the
facts exactly as you found them, where
would I look, class?" No hands. The teacher
glances over at a boy who is surreptitiously
reading a book on astronomy, which is open
on his desk. The teacher snatches the book
from the desktop and holds it in front of the
class. "If I wanted the facts of astronomy
exactly as they are in this book, class, where
would I look?" A few puzzled expressions
and one timidly raised hand. "Sarah?" "You'd
look in that book." "Of course, if I wanted the
facts exactly as you found them I'd look in
the books you found them in. So that means
I want you to do what with the facts, class?"
Several hands are now up, a few of them
shaking vigorously. "Tommy?" "You want us
to say them in our own words." "Yes, of
course. I want you to put them in your own
words. If I wanted to know what the books
say I'd read the books, but I don't. I want to
know what *you* say. So now let's break up
into our committees, and remember, I want

to know what you say and not what the book says. OK?" The children begin to get out of their seats and move their desks to form little clusters of three each. One boy remains sitting alone and the teacher asks him what is wrong. "The other two members of my committee are absent today," he replies. "I'll be over there to help you in just a minute," the teacher promises, and turns to two girls who are standing beside him with an open volume of an encyclopedia held between them.

For the next forty-five minutes the children worked in their committees, chatting quietly together, consulting textbooks and maps. The teacher moved about the room, stopping to talk for a few minutes with some students, glancing appraisingly at the work of others. The atmosphere was relaxed and, with one or two exceptions, the students seemed to be busily engaged in their assignments. At one point the teacher looked at his watch and interrupted the activity long enough to announce that there were twenty minutes remaining in the project period. The students responded to this news with no visible show of either disappointment or pleasure. All in all, it was a model class, as classes go. A supervisor walking in at any time during the morning would likely have been delighted with what he saw, and understandably so. Compared to the conditions existing in many classrooms, where tired and cross teachers are working with inadequate and outdated materials, surrounded by students who have long histories of academic failure, the room in which I sat as a visitor looked like an educational Nirvana.

After the class was over, the teacher and I joined the seminar of educators to discuss the morning session and related matters. At the beginning of the discussion I asked whether the children knew the basis of their selection or knew why they were in school that summer while most of their age peers were out playing ball or building sand castles on the beach. Not only had the issue never been discussed with the students (unless, of course, their parents talked to them about it), but several of the educators thought that it would not be a good idea to bring this matter up in the class. One member of the seminar laughingly said, "Of course the real reason for their being here is to serve as guinea pigs for us! And we couldn't tell them that!"

As the discussion proceeded, it became evident that there were several other matters about which the students had little understanding, in addition to the puzzling question of why they were there in the first place. Although the class had chosen to study fifth-century Rome, the topics on which they were working had been suggested by the teacher. Committee assignments had been made by drawing lots and the size of the committees had been established by dividing the total number of students by the number of topics to be studied. The decision to prepare written reports had been made by the teacher, in consultation with the seminar of educators, so that, as they explained, "the students would have something to show for what they had done." The length of each subject matter period had been set by the teacher, with an eye to achieving some balance in the curriculum.

Certainly few people would argue that the students were being hurt by this experience.

They looked contented enough and, undoubtedly, by the end of the summer they
would know more about fifth-century Rome
than most people know. But the purposeful-
ness of their activity was really quite superficial. No one in the school had bothered to
tell them why they were there, and they
were kept only slightly less in the dark about
what they were studying. In those instances
where the rationale for action was made
clear—as in the definition of committee mem-
bership and size—the underlying principle
turned out not to be rational at all, but simply a matter of chance and convenience.
Even during the opening discussion when
the teacher was trying to bring the students
to the realization that they should personal-
ize their knowledge by casting it in their
own words, the game being played by the
children was the same old one of trying to
guess what the teacher wanted them to say.
Ironically, the object of that little lesson was
almost antithetical to the method used to
achieve it. The one time when the students
were genuinely animated and exploratory
was during their "play" with the musical in-

struments before class. That activity, we will recall, was abruptly terminated so that the real "work" of the day could begin.

This description, I must re-emphasize, is not offered as an example of poor pedagogy, nor as an illustration of the depths to which the forces of mechanization have penetrated the classroom. Had those been my purposes, much more hair-raising descriptions of visits to other schools could easily have been offered. If anything, the classroom described here was better than average and the teacher more resourceful than many I have seen. Yet even there, in a situation relatively free of the institutional constraints that are in operation during the school year, and with students handpicked for their intellectual prowess, the classroom experience, at its core, came close to being dull and meaningless. Many signs of mechanization, as I have defined them, were clearly present. More important, their presence often seemed to be completely unnecessary.

The students' reactions to this state of affairs must be kept firmly in mind. For the most part, they adapted to it without com-

plaint. Indeed, as a group they appeared to
be quite content with their situation. None of
them seemed to wonder why he was asked
to put down his musical instrument, or what
the verse in the Bible meant, or why the
project work period had to end when it did.
Obviously, the answer to all these questions
was "That's just the way school is." The fact
that aspects of their assignment lacked meaning did not seem to prevent them from plug-
ging away at their research and likely doing
a good job of it. Here, then, was a group of
gifted young people who presumably had
learned not to rock the boat when it came to
asking questions about the conditions affecting their daily lives but who, at the same
time, were being urged to adopt a questioning attitude toward the world at large, as
outlined on the blackboard by their teacher.

There is one perspective from which it
probably makes little difference whether or
not students understand what they are doing
and why. This is from the limited view of
education in which the focus is exclusively
on academic achievement. With a better
grasp of why they were there and more ac-

tive participation in the decisions surrounding their work it is doubtful that the students I watched would have wound up
knowing more than they did about fifth-
century Rome. They might even have
learned less because, presumably, they
would have wasted some time discussing
these matters before they got down to the
"real" business of poring over encyclopedia.
Indeed, had they been given a sufficient
amount of freedom and responsibility they
might have decided not to study fifth-
century Rome after all.

As persons responsible for the immediate
well-being of students, as well as for their
future success, educators cannot afford to
focus exclusively on the outcomes of instruction. Particularly, they cannot afford to look
only at the near-at-hand and measurable
residue of classroom work. Students spend
too many hours in school to excuse the obliv-
ion of those in charge to the quality of their
experiences. Despite the popularity of com-
paring medicine with education, going to
school is not at all like going to the doctor's
office where we might wait around an hour

or so to have our sore toe bandaged. Classrooms are comprehensive environments in which a significant portion of our lives are lived—about one thousand hours a year from early childhood through late adolescence. If life there is impoverished and inane, then life in general surely is for the tens of millions whose waking hours are largely spent in classrooms. And this would be so no matter what the scores on achievement tests said, and even if not a single student's voice were raised in protest.

Even if we insist on emphasizing the outcomes of instruction and overlooking the immediate quality of classroom experience, we should not be content with our present methods of assessing the effects of school. If the process of mechanization operates as slowly and as subtly as my observation of the summer class implies, there is no reason to expect the effect on students to be sudden and dramatic. Typically, the educational treatments whose impact we attempt to measure are relatively shortlived—a few days, a month or two, an academic year at most. But what if the treatment lasts much longer and deposits

its sediment at a barely perceptible rate? What if, instead of thinking of schooling as a kind of miracle polish that goes on and comes off in a hurry, leaving a glasslike shine, we began to consider the possibility of its operating like drops of water falling on a stone? Perhaps, if we really wanted to assess the fundamental impact of classroom life, the appropriate interval between our "before" and "after" measurements should not be a few weeks or an academic term, but, rather, a quarter of a lifetime.

Those of us who work in graduate schools frequently experience the sad case of the bright student who gets good grades in all his courses, passes his comprehensive examination with flying colors, and then comes a cropper when it is time to launch out on his own as an independent researcher. Such failures usually have complex roots, and it would be unwise, without further evidence, to lay the blame for them at the steps of the lower schools. Yet I could not help recalling my experiences with some of these graduate students as I watched the summer class of gifted fourth graders. How many of them, I wondered, would face a similar dilemma when they reached young adulthood? How many would become experts at giving the teacher what he wants, but unable to decide what to do when the teacher leaves the room?

If there is a single overarching message behind the speculations offered here, it is that our most pressing educational problem involves learning how to create and maintain a humane environment in our schools. The solution to this problem would seem to require not a narrower look at the anatomy of instruction, but a broader view of what goes on in our classrooms and what can be done to improve them. Opaque projectors, filmstrips, mechanical teaching machines, and even computer consoles may help in the process, but they will not substitute for a firm sense of direction and a commitment to the preservation of human values. Only people come equipped with these qualities. A crucial part of the teacher's job is to see that they continue to do so.